This Is My Confession

This Is My Confession

The Superhero's Tell All
Exclusive Interview!

Shaun Saunders

Shaun Saunders
Hampton, GA

This Is My Confession

The following Bible translations were used in this book: New International Version of the Bible (NIV); The Amplified Bible (AMP); and the English Standard Version of the Bible (ESV).

Cover design by TLH Designs, Chicago, IL (www.tlhdesigns.com)

Book design by Kingdom Living Publishing, Fort Washington, MD (www.kingdomlivingbooks.com)

For information about this book or to contact the author, write to:

Pastor Shaun Saunders
2436 Brianna Dr.
Hampton, GA 30228

You may also send the author an email message at ssaunders89@yahoo.com.

Published by:
Shaun Saunders
Hampton, GA

Published in the United States of America.

ISBN 978-0-692-02244-3

Dedication

To the millions of Superhero leaders around the world who have stumbled and fallen victim to an addiction that continues to harass the innocence of the hero within them.

To the children and youth of our nation, seeking to rediscover the true identity of the Superhero anxiously waiting to be liberated from the confinement of their emotional instabilities and insecurities.

To the families and love ones of Superheroes whom God anointed with the will, patience, resources, and strength to love the hero in the good and the bad.

To Judas, the personality and expression of the ever existing presences of evil cohabitating in the same house with the greatness of the leaders Superhero.

To believers in every city, every town, every state, and every country. It is time for the Real Superheroes to Rise Up! The world is waiting for the real life Avengers to take their place and fight for the well being of all humanity.

Acknowledgments

A book is the picture of the idea that reveals the attitude of the author's heart's desire towards the audience it was intended to capture. In order to ensure that an author's objectives for writing are clearly understood and interpreted appropriately, the content of his message inked throughout the pages of his masterpiece can only be seen through experiences and the countless testimonies of contributors and influencers in his or her life. These individuals, who have through a cooperative process enabled this product to reach millions of people across the world, are the true heroes responsible for the manifestation of this book.

First, I would like to give thanks to my lovely wife, my handsome little boys, and my beautiful baby girls. I really love you guys so much and appreciate you for putting up with daddy's mood swings all throughout the time it took for me to complete this book. If it were not for me waking up to the beauty and joy each of you brings to my life every day, this book would have never become a reality. I love you all so very, very much.

To the Rossi family, I dedicate this book to you in memory of your beloved son, Branden Johnson, aka

Mr. HipStar. Aunt Jennifer, Uncle Nickie, Monique, Angelo, Tony, Necho, and Gino I love you all so much; and we all have been devastated by your loss. Branden, we all miss you, and on behalf of all your friends, family, and fans, I dedicate this book to the life you lived and the legacy you left.

I would like to thank Ms. Irma McKnight and Kingdom Living Publishing for helping with editing and publishing of my book. I would also like to thank TLH Designs for an awesome job designing the book cover.

To all the Superheroes around the world, waiting on one of your fellow heroes to stand up and openly confess the magnitude of a proclivity he has struggled with, and has successfully overcome, this book is especially dedicated to you. Place a demand on the superhero within you to stand up.

Table of Contents

Foreword

Transparency is the key to true freedom. Although it does not always receive the praises of men, it always gains the respect of God. It is only when we come clean with where we are that God can reveal His perfect plan for our lives. Many times, we try to hide our nakedness, but as someone once said, "Confession is good for the soul." Believe it or not, God can handle our mess: *"For we do not have a high priest (Christ), who is unable to sympathize with our weaknesses, but one who in every respect has been tempted as we are, yet without sin"*(ESV).

I applaud Pastor Shaun Saunders for taking such a bold approach in writing this book. It is raw! It is real! It is relevant! Every leader struggles with a dark side that he does not want revealed; however, it is in facing his inner enemy, while pulling and relying on the strength of his inner hero (the Holy Spirit) that brings him victory.

I recommend this book to every leader. It leads one towards self-examination and a sober self-estimation, as well as, promotes the faithfulness of God. I invite you to read, receive, and be free.

Dr. Sonnet Ford-Grant, Founder and Overseer
Divine Impact Christian Outreach Ministries, Int'l

Introduction

This just in! The confession of the highly esteemed, and often times criticized, superhero has shaken up the world. Yes, this once epitomized leader, who revealed to the world his wounds through the eyes of his alter ego, is ready to make an astounding announcement that will leave many of his supporters and critics in shock. Ladies and gentlemen, I must warn you that the nature of this confession contains some graphic images and inappropriate language that may not be suitable for children. So now, I would like to present to you, for the first time ever, this breaking news entitled, *"This is My Confession: The Superhero's Tell All Exclusive Interview."*

Noooooooo! Ashamed and afraid of what those who applauded his possibility might conclude if his secret were to escape into the hands of those who specialize in killing their wounded, the disguise of the Superhero's undercover identity has been compromised. Now the evolution of the monster he denied existed has been exposed, leaving the once indestructible leader in the awkward position of explaining the unexplainable to an audience with varying opinions. Drowning in his tears, regretting the missed opportunities to connect with the one or two individuals willing to avail themselves to his sickness, he stands to his feet, quivering frantically as one possessed by the chill of death; ready to confirm the reality of the man hiding in the closet. Still believing in the possibility of declaring his innocence in the presence of those who openly encourage the recovery of saints shackled by their calamity, he admittedly seeks to provide for himself a logical explanation that will justifiably expel him from the consequences of his disease.

As the evidence surrounding the Superhero's case is gathered, and the facts are made available for all those inside and outside the comforts of his inner circle to hear, he, under the guilt and condemnation of his affliction, attempts to confess the extent of his premeditated involvement in this unimaginable, but common sin. As he approaches the platform, prepared to expose the world to his nastiness, crowds filled with both haters and supporters of the wounded leader stand anxious to hear his confession. With an overwhelming chant of his haters saying, "I told you so" coupled with the extremely low and fading chant of "We still believe in you," the Superhero approaches the red carpet and begins his long journey down the walk of shame. His face now flooded with tears and humility the only available crutch left for him to stand on, he stumbles shamefully to the podium to address his audience:

Ladies and gentlemen, today I have come to share with you a sin I have been struggling with for a long time. It is with great sorrow and joy that I have come before you today. I know that some will use my confession as a means to justify continuing in sin, but others will be encouraged to confess their struggles and seek out God's help. So today, on this October 29, I confess that I, that I struggle with ....

As he searched for the words that would eloquently minimize the weight and the continuity of his consensual involvement with a sin God never asked him to explain but only to confess, he speaks in a coded dialect that will provide him with enough wiggle room to escape the rebellion of an audience critical of his behavior. With a barrage of intellectual words, void of any credible and verifiable substance, his supposed confession becomes the voice of sarcasm to an audience he presumes to be ignorant and unlearned. "What? Oh no he didn't just try and play me like a fool!" a faithful supporter shouts, threatened by the empty apology of the hero, she was convinced God chose to love and care for her soul. As the anger of the expectant crowd furiously burns, insulted by the hero's lethargic declarations, the limited momentum of the presenter quickly begins to swing in the favor of his naysayers.

Facing the inevitable uprising of a ferocious crowd and the unbearable reality of conquering a sin from which he would like to hide, he contemplates quenching the fire of God he feels shut up in his bones with the sacrifice of his life. Yes, suicide! Overwhelmed with the guilt of his sin, compiled with his insidious thoughts and a hostile audience, he fearfully seeks after the opportunity to relieve himself of the secret silently killing his hero from within.

Deeply woven within the fabric of a hero's autobiographical sketch is the shame every hero, at one time or another wished they could eliminate from their history of their story. The psalmist in Psalm 90:8 (AMP) says, *"Our iniquities, our secret heart and its sins {which we would so like to conceal even from ourselves}, You have set in the {revealing} light of Your countenance."*

The Superhero's willingness to expose a sin that he has unsuccessfully mastered is an invitation backstage into the dressing room of the makeup less personality hiding behind the mask of the character his fans love to admire. The Superhero's unattractive posture, or what the apostle Paul would call the thorn in the Superhero's flesh, is the kryptonite that paralyzes the hero's inner Rocky Balboa, penetrating his indestructible frame with a lethal force. With his weakness now exposed and his reputation destroyed, the possibility of the Superhero's potential has been disqualified due to his illegal use of an addiction that obscures his will to pursue an idea he no longer believes can be obtained. With all hope lost, it appears that the end of the Superhero's fantasy is an inevitable reality.

Could this really be the end of the Superhero saga? Will the illustrious hall of fame career of the Superhero, who could do no wrong, become tainted with accusations of inappropriate behavior, accusations given by the freak he exiled from the history of his story? Will he openly confess and explain the details of his extreme nastiness? Or will he say, in the infamously famous words of R. Kelly, "It wasn't me," in the surveillance video that clearly identifies him as the primary suspect at the scene of the crime? What will the Superhero do? Ladies and gentlemen, I present to you the answers to these questions in my new book entitled, *This is My Confession: The Superhero's Tell All Exclusive Interview!*

Chapter One

An ESPN Highly Publicized Event: A Superhero's Decision!

As the urgency arises in the hearts of zealous supporters, an atmosphere once conditioned with the possibility of achieving the impossible has been silenced by the rumored infidelity of a Superhero, who failed to deliver on a promise he guaranteed. The emotional instability of an energized fan base—fans faithfully devoted to a mandated mission—intensifies as the loyalty of the "chosen one" turns into a thriller that chills the aspirations of those anxious to hear where the Superhero stands regarding the continuity of their relationship. Now exhausted, due to the emotional rollercoaster ride of a capricious Superhero, fans stand in denial, saying what they need to hear hoping to convince themselves that he is sure to remain forever a committed companion to what they believe is a monogamous relationship. In an attempt to persuade the hero that no one else will love him as they do, crowds, with their candles lit, echoed the lyrics of a song to their beloved, singing with a sparkle in their eyes "Baby won't you just stay?" As he makes his decision on an ESPN Highly Publicized Event entitled *The Decision* to take his talents to South Beach and partner with his alter ego, formulating a highly talented, but hated dynamic duo, the outcome all of his loyal followers feared the most has come upon them. Like a Jewish leader crying out enthusiastically for the release of Barabbas, hoping to justify the crucifixion of an innocent Savior, the memory of the good the "Chosen One" was able to perform in their presence has been erased by the resurrection and betrayal of his Judas. Judas Iscariot, the disciple who betrayed Jesus for thirty pieces of silver, is in the context of Scripture the epitome of evil existing within the presence of the chosen one.

> *"Then one of the Twelve—the one called Judas Iscariot—went to the chief priests and asked, "What are you willing to give me if I deliver Him over to you?" So they counted out for him thirty pieces of silver. From then on Judas watched for an opportunity to hand Him over"* (Matthew 26:14-16 (NIV)).

Similar to Jesus, every Superhero anointed with supernatural strength is also endowed, unfortunately, with a potentially lethal dose of kryptonite released through the personality of their internalized Judas, who ferociously seeks the right occasion to cripple the superhero's power with a deadly kiss. In the book of Psalms, King David announces, *"Even my close friend, someone I trusted, one who shared my bread has turned against me"* (Psalm 41:9 (NIV)).

What does a leader do when the king in him is seduced by the lust of his betrayer, cohabitating in the same house and sleeping in the same bed as his Superhero? How can the Superhero get up when he is struck with a blow to the belly by a weakness that hinders his ability to stand up straight?

Judas is that illusive monster, considered to be the darker of the two personalities identified within the superhero's portfolio. As his schizophrenic posture accentuates the complexity of an addiction that continues to resurface, in his present reality, this freak that comes out at night tries to assault the anointing of his hero with the alluring appeal of a generational lust that promises pleasures that will never satisfy. So just who is this Judas? The name *Judas* means "Praise of The Lord." It is similar to the name *Judah* in Hebrew. His surname, *Iscariot,* means "Man of Kerioth" or "A Man of Murder." He was the last of the 12 Jesus called to the office of apostle and granted the admirable duty of working as the chief financial officer during his tenure under Jesus' administration. His works are the epitome of a rebellious superhero exemplifying a lack of confidence in the finished work of a Perfect God. Superheroes sometimes forget that their work is a corresponding action that affirms the authenticity of their confidence. The hardest work they will ever have to do in life is the work of surrendering their will over to, or submitting their will up under, the perfect will of their Heavenly Father. They do not work to win, because Jesus has already won the battle for them. No, they work to reveal the winner between the forces of good and evil, battling over who has inherited the right to influence their internal and exterior posture. So then Judas is the spiritually unstable body of work Satan enters into to express the physical posture of a relentless evil synonymously cohabitating with the greater good found within the core of the Superhero's inner circle. Like Jesus, a Superhero must maintain an admirable posture, never projecting any emotional instability or malicious contempt towards his internalized evil. Despite His foreknowledge of the conspiracy plotted against Him—a conspiracy finalized by the inevitable betrayal of the one He called friend—Jesus never denounced Judas. Rather, He expected Judas to embrace his role as the villain, the confrontational character God strategically positioned him to be in the history of the Jesus story. Jesus' poise under pressure exemplifies the strength of a leader abstaining from criticizing his Judas for his contemptuous behavior, by continuing to reveal himself as a close friend, despite the tragedy of his opponent's deception:

"Going at once to Jesus, Judas said, "Greetings, Rabbi!" and kissed Him. Jesus replied, "Do what you came for, FRIEND" (Matthew 26:49b-50 (NIV)).

By seeing Judas in the capacity in which the Father created him, and not expecting him to be any more or less than what his Father said he should be, Jesus methodically placed His diabolical nemesis in the awkward position of being overwhelmed with the guilt of his betrayal:

When Judas, who had betrayed Him, saw that Jesus was condemned, he was seized with remorse and returned the thirty pieces of silver, to the chief priests and the elders. "I have sinned," he said "For I have betrayed innocent blood." So Judas threw the money into the temple and left. Then he went away and hanged himself (Matthew 27: 3-4b (NIV)).

It is clear here that Jesus' ability to continue to acknowledge Judas as a friend, in light of his betrayal, was a calculated attempt to place the son of perdition in the uncomfortable position of seeing the consequences of his decision for himself. Notice, Jesus never plotted to kill Judas. Judas killed himself as a result of Jesus' immutability or his unwillingness to change his perception of him after his fall. Real superheroes never plot to excommunicate their Judas, but when confronted by his resistance, they place his spiritually unstable body under an anointing that will cause him to turn violently on himself. Every attempt a Superhero takes to kill his Judas is an act of submission over to the role his Judas personality has scripted for the hero to play in his fantasy. The Superhero must corner Judas with an empathetic embrace that will cause him, without the efforts of the hero's powers, to silence himself.

The significance of Judas' posture, actively employed within the historical context of the Superhero saga, confirms the always existing presence of evil residing in an abundance of the superhero's highly notable accomplishments. The apostle Paul says it like this in the book of Romans:

> *"For I do not do the good I want to do, but the evil I do not want to do—this I keep on doing. Now if I do what I do not want to do, it is no longer I who do it, but it is sin living in me that does it. So I find this law at work: Although I want to do good EVIL IS RIGHT THERE WITH ME'* (Romans 7:19-21 (NIV)).

Now wrestling with whether or not to concede to the notion that relegates the existence of an often-intense natural inclination to perform under the influence of an illusion deeply woven within a space of time called opportunity, the Superhero struggles to embrace the dark side of an evil that promises to be forever in opposition to his destiny. With an expulsion no longer a possibility, the Superhero, similar to a special education teacher, must develop an Individual Evaluation Plan (IEP) to help him break free from a label placed on him, due to his spontaneous display of uncontrolled erratic behavior that will always define his future by who he was and not by whom God declared he is. Pornography, masturbation, adultery, molestation, murder, lying, alcoholism, prostitution, or yes what most would say is the coup de grâce of them all, homosexuality, are all channels that project tangible expressions of the always existing presence of evil employed to persuade superheroes to surrender their will over to the aspirations of their Judas. The focus with which the Superhero attempts to shield himself from the villainous character his Judas has scripted for him to portray in his illusion is the driving force that energizes his body to conform to an immoral pattern of behavior that he has so forcefully tried all his life to avoid.

Whenever a Superhero focuses his time, energy, and efforts on not yielding his body over to any of those unlawful expressions mentioned above, he decapitates the head of his hero while at the same time crowning Judas as the ruler and king of his life. Criticizing Judas will never stagger his momentum, but rather continue to sponsor him with additional airtime that will enable him to promote further his "sketchy" agenda. It is amazing to me that before the 2012 Presidential Election the Incumbent, President Barack Obama, and his challenger, Governor Mitt Romney, spent over 1 billion dollars in attack ads, hoping to disqualify each other in the eyes of voters. The mutual disdain both candidates had for each other was the facade they hid behind to energize their base and the platform they used to suggest to independent voters that they were the lesser of two evils. Loaded with sharp criticisms, pervasive talking points, flip-flopping, and say anything to get elected politics, both of the presidential prospects decided to campaign on their opponent's incompetencies, without ever clearly projecting to their voting audience an authentic reflection of who they were, who they are, and what they promised they would be if elected. In similar fashion, a Superhero's undermining rationale—his unlawful conviction that seeks to justify a false sense of entitlement—is a distraction he employs to disguise his vulnerabilities, by zealously criticizing the weaknesses of anyone capable of compromising his cover.

Threatened by the possibility of being subjected to the involuntary exposure of the evil of which he continues to convince himself he was unaware, the Superhero's projections of what he was and the possibility of his potential to become are manipulated by his fear of being perceived as a failure in the eyes of a fickle audience. His desire to become what the wayward thoughts of a fickle audience have challenged him to be places him in an unfavorable condition to which he is destined to fail. It is here, while in distress, confused about how to proceed, that the Superhero's weakness reveals itself as the catalyst that dramatically stimulates his undiscovered supernatural ability to overcome, affirming the durability of his strength when threatened by the possibility of defeat. Failure is the inevitable reality with which every leader at some point in their life will have to become acquainted. It is not always the equivalent of a loss or weakness, but rather a potential pathway to Godly success. Loss or weakness should never be considered a threat, but rather an opportunity to validate the quality of strength residing in whatever designated substance it was assigned specifically to torment. It is only when leaders acknowledge and embrace their weakness, the expression of their Judas, that they will be able to expose the true origin of their strength. According to an old Chinese Proverb, "Failure is not falling down, but refusing to get back up." For leader's, it is refusing to reconnect with the true origin of their strength that empowers them to get back up again. The apostle Paul says in 2 Corinthians 12:7b-10 (NIV):

> *"I was given a thorn in my flesh, a messenger of Satan to torment me. Three times I pleaded with the Lord to take it away from me. But He (Jesus) said to me, My grace is sufficient for you, for My power is made perfect in weakness.* ***Therefore will I boast all the more gladly about my weaknesses, so that Christ power may rest on me.*** *That is why, for Christ's sake, I delight in weakness, in insults, in hardships, in persecutions, in difficulties.* ***For when I am weak, then I am strong."***

The apostle Paul goes on later to say in the fourth chapter of the book of Philippians, *"I can do all things through Him (Christ) who gives me strength"* (Philippians 4:13 (NIV)).

A weakness then is a measure used to enlighten the Superhero to either the sufficiency or insufficiency of the source from which he relies for his strength. A Superhero's will to win is meaningless without the additional strength needed to perform up to the expectations of a desire he was destined to fulfill. The astounding image of the Superhero sitting unashamedly at a prepared table, in the presence of his most fierce enemy, himself, is the unfolding of a beautiful scene directed by God, starring the Superhero and the always-existing presence of his internal Judas.

God never prepares a table, for the Superhero, in the presence of his enemy (Judas) to test the quality of his strength, but rather for the Superhero to become reacquainted with the strength and sovereignty of God, with which he must learn to depend. This principle can be more clearly understood in Genesis 22. God's request for Abraham, the Superhero in the context of this story, to sacrifice his only begotten son was not a test for an omniscient God to see whether or not Abraham would be faithful, but rather an opportunity for God to show Abraham that He is faithful.

It is impossible for the origin of the Superhero's strength, due to its extraordinary irregularity, ever to be mistaken for anything but a manifestation of supernatural power. His strength supplier irrevocably seeks only to expose the Superhero to the continuity of his sufficiency challenging him to abandon all other possible sources and compelling him to depend only on him as the primary supplier of the power he demands. Unfortunately, due to the barrage of false advertisers pretending to authenticate their power as the most valuable source of energy available for the Superhero to depend for strength, the Superhero is faced with the difficult decision of deciding which source will strengthen him to reproduce the effectively efficient product God has always enabled him to supply continually.

When the Superhero decides to reconnect with the right source of energy he was originally and with which he was previously acquainted, success will become an undeniable reality endorsed by the testimony of both the light in his Man of Steel and the darkness in his inner Judas. Will he, however, continue to pledge his allegiance to a power he has tested, tried, and proven? Or will he snuggle up in the arms of one of his ex-lovers and take a dive into the panties of an adulterous affair with a former flame unable to support the weight of his destiny? Will he flirt with the instability and insufficiency of his own strength? Or will he denounce all others and totally confide in the only power capable of enhancing his performance?

As the plot thickens and the thin line between the true origin of his strength and the simplicity of his weakness are identified more clearly, the Superhero must decide on which of the two testimonies he will trust to catch him when he falls from the tightrope of life. With no alibi, and the eyewitness testimony from both his good and evil sides, critics determine the Superhero to be the primary suspect at the scene of the crime and have warned his fans to stay away because he is considered to be armed and dangerous. Now on the brink of an emotional collapse, torn between sharing his truth, and his whole truth, with a very disgruntled fan base, the Superhero openly seeks to confess the extent of his involvement in this unexpected scandal in his tell all exclusive interview with the Daily Times most diabolical reporter, The Accuser of the Brethren!

Chapter Two

This Is My Confession: The Superhero's Tell-All Exclusive Interview with the Daily Times Most Diabolical Reporter, the Accuser!

Testing, testing! Microphone check one, two! As the skilled and highly qualified technicians adjust their volume levels during a pre-exclusive interview sound check, fans and critics gather in long lines outside of the studio where the third confrontation between the Superhero and the Daily Times most diabolical reporter, the Accuser, will finally take place. Some analysts have projected that this "Thriller in Manila" will capture a glimpse of reality TV at its best. Filled with excitement, similar to the excitement surrounding the possibility of a Floyd "Money" Mayweather fight with the Filipino Kid, Mr. Manny "Packman" Pacquaio, a fight that may have taken place if Pacquaio had not gotten knocked the hell out in his last fight by Juan Manuel Marquez, most of the Superhero's critics predict that the pay per view ratings for this highly publicized tell all exclusive interview will reach unprecedented levels. Audiences of various ethnicities, persuasions, sexes, social classes, religions, addictions, handicaps, and sin preferences have once again rekindled their romance for the reemergence of a historic feud that caused many of the sport's die-hard fans to lose interest because of its absence. Like an echo from the Michael Jackson "Bad Album," the Accuser hypes the fight on his Twitter account, tweeting to the Superhero, "He ain't bad!" For months, both parties have subjected themselves to a rigorous training schedule to prepare for what they are sure will be a fight to the death. Tensions burn as the interviewer and the interviewee stand toe-to-toe, eyeball-to-eyeball, muscle-to-muscle during the pre-interview weigh in, fueling the anxiety of onlookers to tune in to what, at first glance, appears to be an unevenly matched bout.

In the last bout between these two fighters, the Superhero was TKO'd by the current heavyweight champion, the Accuser, with a lethal combination of punches. With the devastating jab of perversion, the exhausting body shot of pornography, and the deceptively powerful and effective uppercut of idolatry, each of the Superhero's losses have disastrously projected an image of him in the memory of his opponent that narrows the possibility of his victory by projecting, on the basis of their history, the inevitable likelihood of his defeat. As the time draws near to the main event and both fighters walk through their prefight rituals, the excitement of those privileged to sit ringside is ignited by the spark of an announcer eager to introduce the champion and the challenger as they, escorted by a large entourage, approach the battleground.

Now with the fighters' ringside, and the lights all around the stands in the arena slowly fading into the darkness, the intensity shifts to the drama that will unfold under the bright lights drawing the attention of a divided audience to the center of the ring. Ding, Ding, Ding! With the ring of the bells, the announcer makes the introductions, and the fighters are accompanied by their corners to the center of the ring for one last meet and greet with the referee to reiterate the rules by which both fighters have promised to abide.

After the fighters have been sworn in, promising to tell the whole truth, and nothing but the truth so help them God, touching gloves and marching back to their corners, the ESPN ringside announcers calling the fight notify fans that the thoughts of each of the fighters have been wired for sound, allowing the viewing audience to examine on a big screen either the progression or digression of their thinking throughout the duration of this battle. Neither of the two considers themselves products of their environment, but rather products of their thoughts. The demeanor they display within the confines of this competitive environment they have managed to create is the mirror that will project a more telling image of how they feel and what they think about themselves and each other. The words fighters usually use to describe themselves often conflict with the ideal image of the man they truly think they are. Scriptures says that whatsoever a man thinks he is, not what he says he is, so is he. Like those ten foolish Israelite spies in Numbers 13 who said, *"We seemed like grasshoppers in our own eyes, and we looked the same to them,"* this fight will compare the execution of each fighter's thoughts by the integrity of their performance.

It has finally come down to the moment we have all been waiting for. As fans await the sound of the bell, the energy surrounding the ring where the two will get it on has reached a twenty on a scale with a maximum measure of ten. Ding, Ding! With the sound of the bell, the fighters violently engage in a malicious exchange. In an attempt to assert himself as the aggressor, the Accuser, who had predicted an early round knockout, throws a combination of questions at the Superhero, backing him into a corner and staggering his momentum. Pounding him with a fierce combination of body blows, the Accuser hits the Superhero with the first question jab to the head causing him to stumble. Exhausting most of his energy in the early rounds, the Accuser asks, "If you truly are a Superhero, can you please, for once in your life, give the specifics of your struggle publicly and expose the world to the nakedness of an addiction you once were or possibly still are ashamed of?"

As the Accuser continues to inflict his will on the Superhero, taunting him with explicit and emasculating language, the Superhero leans back on the ropes in a fighting posture more commonly identified as the Muhammad Ali rope-a-dope. He positions himself in a protected stance to experience the thrill of victory, by first exposing himself to the agony of defeat. Up against the ropes, hammered with a barrage of questions, that seems to come one after the other, the Superhero allows the Accuser to hit him time after time, causing his opponent to punch himself out, forcing him into making a mistake that the Superhero can then exploit in a counterattack.

With a similar Feng shui as the seventh degree Aikido black belt master, Steven Segal, the Superhero blends his fighting style with the motion of his attacker and redirects the force of his opponent's energy rather than trying to oppose him head on. If he can endure the punishment he has had to endure so far, his plan to use the Accuser's momentum against him may allow him to regain his title. Unlike the naivety of Notre Dame middle linebacker Manti Te'o, hoaxed into glamorizing the beauty of the beloved dead girlfriend that never ever existed, or the arrogantly calculated confession of a bullish lying seven time Tour de France winner, doped up for years on performance enhancement drugs forced into having a come-to-Jesus moment with Oprah, the Superhero has elected by his own free will to disguise his strength quietly by unashamedly encouraging his opponent to attack a weakness that he will voluntarily expose.

Round after round, the Superhero subjects himself to a brutal interrogation, while still taunting the champion with, "Hit me with your best shot," as he waits for his opponent to slip up with a question that will allow him to respond at just the right moment with a knockout answer. After several rounds of serving a five to ten minute hard time sentence, five to ten minutes of getting his butt kicked, the Superhero finally decides to man up and retaliates with a devastating blow of an answer that leaves the accuser and his haters speechless.

With an awl striking shout of "Stop," the momentum in an atmosphere once considered to be a more favorable advantage for the opposition unexpectedly begins to shift in favor of the Superhero. Like the unorthodox rapping style of an MC better known as "Rabbit," who, on his way back up to the "8-Mile," left one of the most feared battle lyrist of his time, the Don, Papa Dock, on stage lifeless with an unusual description of himself to which he ends with a challenge to his opponent to tell the people something they didn't know about him, the Superhero flips the script on the interviewer with his lightening quick hand speed and a fight changing poetic dissertation.

As the Superhero warrior finally begins to put his mark on the fight, an audio recording of the Superhero's thoughts is confiscated by an anonymous hater determined to bear false witness against the transformation of the Superhero's renewed mind. Loaded with what he believes to be potentially damaging evidence, the anonymous hater releases the Superhero's recorded thoughts to the press in exchange for thirty pieces of silver. The following is an exclusive audio recording of a conversation the Superhero had with himself, capturing the evolution of his thinking throughout the duration of the interview:

> "I am guilty as charged! As the primary suspect in the murder of the Superhero in me, I confess that I am the epitome of the father that I hated. Yes, I have struggled with pornography, looked at other women lustfully, and projected publicly the image of a man I am not privately. I am the product of my father's fathers' mistake. I hate you; no, I hate me. You, Judas, the ever existing presence of my evil betrayer living within me, have intrigued me to lust after a proclivity that continues emasculating me from the evolution of my maleness causing me to neglect the responsibility of my manhood. You have castrated my father, his father, and my father's fathers' father; you have convinced me to squabble in isolation with a thorn that continues to express itself through the corrupted flesh of my family pedigree.
>
> My efforts not to become the freak you have determined to prove I am deceived me into becoming the expression of habit that I hate and

despise. Honestly, I would much rather fight with my external Goliath than to deal with the self inflicted pain of a wound I received in a fight with you, no me, no with myself. I was just as nasty as I wanted to be, had no integrity, no stability, and was manipulated by a fear of you exposing my inadequacy. Because I was addicted to your promises of pleasure that never once satisfied my yearning, I underestimated you and quantified your testimony as impermissible evidence in the defense of my success.

Now sinking in my sin, my mind branded with the mark of a beast that without any notification spontaneously decides to show up like herpes, I continue to debate with you over whether or not there is any resolve that would provide me a way of escape from this egregious dis-ease. Then finally, at what I presumed to be the lowest of my lowest points, at the point when I was ready to give up, it happened!

I met a man I thought I knew and he reintroduced me to the man, the hero, I thought my disease automatically disqualified me from becoming. He rescued me, cleaned me up and out, and reminded me that out of all the hell I have done, still am doing, and may do in the future, if I repent, the only sins he will remember are the sins of which I continue to remind him. As a matter of fact, he mentioned you and told me to tell you, "Thank You!" Thank you for re-introducing us.

If it had not been for you, it is possible we may have never met again. Oh Judas, yes you, the ever existing presence of evil living within me, have you forgotten already? Well, allow me to reintroduce you to and reacquaint you with that someone who exposed the world to those undeniable dirty little truths about you. He was your first and the most significant of all the recipients of your betrayal. Seduced by the power of His accuser, you placed the kiss of your idolatrous lips on His cheek successfully culminating your assignment within the history of His story.

In your efforts to justify your misconduct that led to His death, you have conspired along with rebel forces aspiring to sabotage His innocence by terrorizing the faith of the superhero that abides in the soul of those individuals He has specifically anointed with special powers to reveal the details of a will that He has already fulfilled. You thought the grass was greener on the other side. Only when it was too late did you come to realize that because your view had been obscured by the distance existing between the points from where you were standing and to where you were lusting, the grass over there was not at all what it was advertised to be. For thirty pieces of silver, you exchanged your soul for His life and as a result of your behavior concluded that it probably was ***cheaper to keep Him.*** Unable to right the wrong that you did to Him, you, from the time of your betrayal of Him, have continued to show your insubordination towards the heroes, in whom He lives and has appointed to lead today. Though the names in the stories may have changed, the results are still the same. You Lose! When you lost to Him over 2,000 years ago and He won, I won too. I have always crowned you, my Judas, with the title of my worst enemy, but you never were. I finally realize now that my worst enemy has always been and will always be me. Like you did in His day, you came into the presence of my inner circle, entered into the ever existing presence of my evil Judas and you watched and waited for an opportunity to hand the JESUS in me over to the accuser when no crowd was present. You are the birthmark I thought I could remove, a constant reminder of a weakness that accompanied me in my conception.

You are the swinging door I forgot to check, left unlocked, an unrestricted point of entry for the Accuser to broadcast his doubts about me. You, however, forgot one thing. Jesus and I are one, making it virtually impossible for you to distinguish between the two of us. When you betrayed Him with that idolatrous kiss, you betrayed me. Your indulging obsession and indelible infatuation with me are reminders of your regret in the betrayal of His innocence that will remain forever embedded in your memory.

The re-emergence of the Superhero in me is a constant reminder of the guilt you felt in that moment when you realized the magnitude of your mistake. You still long for an escape from the antagonizing remorse you have continued to struggle with, applied by the pressure of his unexpected declaration of you as a friend.

Your jealously is the motivation behind your reason for stopping me. You are the greatest of all my enemies and ranked highest among my haters. So today, I salute you with a hello, from a man whose name is higher than any other name. He is the answer that allows me to distance the Superhero in me from the residue of the freakiness I indulged in when I followed after you. He is the reason why, after you have humiliated me, insulted me, afflicted me, beat me, betrayed me, and tried to kill me, I continue to get up from my fall with my mind and body transformed from the bruises of your punches into the image of His reflection. See, now I got my mind right, money right; and I am ready for war. Finally, it is my turn to inflict pain on you with one fatal blow to the head called ***THE ALL DAY JESUS UPPERCUT.***

With his thoughts now projected on the big screen for both his haters and appreciators to observe, the once marginalized and ostracized superstar begins to move around the ring with a redemptive swagger that confuses his unsuspecting opponent. Like the little rigid Shepherd boy, David, who with a slingshot and one smooth stone demoralized what King Saul presumed to be an unbeatable giant, the Superhero with one punch breaks the neck of the Accuser and his erroneous accusations, killing him softly with his words, causing his body to go into neurogenic shock. As you will see, instant replay captures a glimpse of the Accuser's last thought, right before and during his flight up and back down to the canvas, where his body lays lifeless. We must warn you that this footage is very graphic in nature, but we highly recommend that superheroes all over the world listen and frantically rejoice over the fall of the Accuser. As the referee goes under the hood to look and see if the punch that landed on the Accuser's chin was a legal blow, fans watch and listen to the replay of his thoughts on the stadium's Jumbotron LCD video screen.

'Ahhhhhhhhhhhhhhhhhhh! I have been waiting for this moment. Then, just when it's about to end, he opened up and said to me, "You no longer are the champion." This fool, he doesn't know who I am. I'll eat him up and spit him out again. With an uppercut to my chin, my knees buckle and I start wobbling. Oh, I feel my body paralyzed, urine running down my thighs. Wait, isn't he supposed to be afraid of me? I think he's come to recognize I'm full of crap and full of lies; no need for me ever to deny the power in his uppercut made me cry out, "Jesus, Whyyyyyy!" Now I'm laying on the ground, knocked out. I want to scream and I want to shout. I'm lying down with my belly out and blood running from my mouth. No, this is not the end of me; I'll wait for another opportunity to shatter all his confidence with a sin that will allow me to rob him of his innocence. But honestly, he caught me with a good one; but he won't ever catch me with another one. This interview is finished and done. It's over; I lost and he won.

Chapter Three

The Test: On the Other Side of Victory!

As the lights slowly fade into the silence and the other side of victory begins to assert itself as an obtained reality, the Superhero exits to the left of the ring after a late round knockout of the Accuser to meet with members of the press for his post fight interview. Following the direction of the ringside coordinator, he is led into a dark room void of the fanatical zeal of his fans that usually precedes a champion's triumphant processional to the podium for a question and answer session with reporters. "What the hell!" He yells out. Expecting to be rushed by a throng of fans pressing him for his autograph, he is instead greeted by a hush and the quietness of nobody calling his name. Under the impression his victory automatically earned him a seat among the elite, similar to a police officer carefully looking through a suspect's house to take him into custody, his search of the area where he prematurely assumed a party in his behalf would be going down was empty, swept clean of any evidence that would verify the whereabouts of all those invited to his after party bash. In his frustration, he renders an expression that captures a glimpse of his arrogance declaring openly, for his own comfort in the absence of all confirmation, "I am the Champion now, I can't be beat." Faced with the new reality of success to which he obviously did not prepare himself ahead of time, the Superhero's journey into this unfamiliar territory has convinced him that he is entitled to a pat on the back that will culminate his inauguration into the company of those who have apprehended. Unlike the apostle Paul who in Philippians chapter three verse twelve said, *"Not that I have already obtained all this, or have already arrived at my goal, but I press on to take hold of that for which Christ Jesus took hold of me,"* the valiant Superhero champion arrogantly sits in the contentment of his own glory only to be introduced to the daunting realization that obtaining the reward he so violently pursued does not always satisfy the hunger and thirst used to motivate and inspire him to pursue after his goal.

The Superhero's inability to disassociate seizing his primary objective from the success of conquering his ultimate goal has caused him to prematurely celebrate the end of war with his enemy, after only winning one battle. Does he not know that one win does not make him a winner? Is a millionaire a millionaire because he has a million dollars? No, but he is a millionaire because of his ability to continue to produce more millions. Thrilled by the emotions of his victory he, under the umbrella of uncertainty, begins to speak more highly of himself than he should, hoping to reassure himself of his ability to continue to produce victorious results at a championship level.

Now on the other side of victory he begins to embellish himself with the aura of a champion, without ever defending his title, failing to prepare himself for a rematch with an opponent whom he must have forgotten is a spiritual terrorist. The fanaticism and zeal of a spiritual terrorist are never expressed through the miniscule loss of a battle, but only in the fear of a continuous threat of war in the places where the Superhero looks for comfort and predictability. Like the skepticism of the serpent in Genesis chapter three, a spiritual terrorist's primary objective is to destroy the Superhero's confidence in the safety of the places he was anointed to occupy by feeding him with fear through the hero's insecurity in the only place he once felt secure.

The Accuser will obediently subject himself to a loss while allowing the Superhero to win the battle, only to surprise him with a continuum of unexpected attacks in places of comfort, prematurely exposing the Superhero to a culture manipulated by false expectations that appear to be real. Now afraid that he might never excel to what he presumes to be the highest pinnacle of success, the Superhero places a death grip hold on his championship belt, afraid that he might not be able to reproduce again the same results that he once was able to produce in himself before. Desiring to sit in the comfort of the spotlight he mistakenly assumed would accompany his victory, the Superhero focuses on establishing his credibility under the pressure of his presumed fame. Intent on living his life like it's golden, he consumes himself with himself and being deceived by his own self-righteousness expects to be served rather than serve others. Simply blinded by the glare of his self-proclaimed fame, as so many other one-hit wonders or a rap artist who gives all praise to God in his award winning acceptance speech for a song full of explicit and misogynistic lyrics towards women, the Superhero, like a child prodigy from the Disney channel, trades in his childlike innocence for the extremely provocative and seductively unpredictable world of fame.

It is important to note that a hero's ill-advised pursuit after fame is not a necessity, but rather a desire for him to hear God say it is okay for him to have something God never said it was okay for him to have. This is why most Christian believers believe that God does not respond to their prayers. God always responds to prayer, just maybe not in a way we would like. No response from God is a response. The Word of God is not called the Speaking Word, it is called the Spoken Word. Every word we hear when God speaks is the echo of a word that He has spoken before. The leader's heart is the surface He uses to reproduce the repetitious sound of a word that He spoke before. So a true Godly leader never suggest that what God is saying now is something hc has never said before, but reiterates and reinforces what God has already spoken.

The leader's deception in praying for what he wants and not for what God said he could have has caused many to assume that God is unresponsive to their prayers. Psalm 37:4 says, *"Take delight in the Lord, and He will give you the desires of your heart."* It is simple; when you delight yourself in God, you will desire for yourself those things He, in His heart, has always desired for you to have. When we pray outside of His will, He ignores our request and responds to our motive for asking. Sometimes in prayer, believers are unaware of the true motivation behind why they ask God to bless them with what they asked for. Because he is more concerned with the intentions behind the action, He seeks to uncover the truth of the believer's intent that caused him to make his unwarranted request.

God always responds to prayer by exposing the petitioner to the condition of their heart to help them clearly understand and appreciate whatever response He gives as an answer to their prayers. When believers pray, they need to ask God according to what He said and not what they desire for Him to say:

> *"This is the confidence we have in approaching God: that if we ask anything according to his will, he hears us-whatever we ask-we know that we have what we asked of him"* (1 John 5:14 (NIV)).

Believers are supposed to be leaders who always pray for what they need. Some would suggest that when the Lord appeared at night to Solomon in a dream and told him to ask for whatever he wanted the Lord to give him, that this was an open-ended question. However, it was not. There was only one answer that Solomon could have given that was correct. And Solomon answered correctly: *"So give your servant a discerning heart to govern Your people and to distinguish between right and wrong"* (1 Kings 3:9 (NIV)).

As a result of asking for what he needed, God not only promised to provide him with what he asked for, but also with those things he desired but did not mention: *Moreover, I will give you what you have not asked for-both wealth and honor-so that in your lifetime you will have no equal among kings* (2 Kings 3:13 (NIV)).

The ignorance of the unlearned has caused many leaders to first seek after what they want as opposed to gathering around themselves the needed resources to ensure a harmonious union between what's needed and the unnecessary. It is impossible for the Superhero to prioritize his motivation appropriately to pursue after something he wants without a continual supply of the resources he needs. Solomon's answer for wisdom to lead God's people may not have been what he desired, but at that time, it was what he needed. Therefore, because Solomon desired for himself what God desired for him to have, God not only gave him what he desired, but also the things he did not ask for, enabling him with his needs met to maintain, correctly monitor, and make wise decisions concerning the accelerated value of his wants on his list of priorities. It is essential to note here the insignificance of the Superhero asking God to bless him with what he wants without first providing him with what he will need to display outwardly God's wisdom on how to use, to God's advantage, those things he wants, but does not necessarily need.

Marinating in the nostalgia of his victory, the Superhero, absent of all the publicity that would usually accompany his success, quickly comes to learn that a leader's success does not exempt him from the responsibility of retaining the victory's crown. The true test of every champion is not winning when he is expected to lose, but maintaining his poise under pressure, continuing to win when he is expected to win. A true champion also reveals his superiority to his opponent when he is faced with what appears to be an insurmountable obstacle, but always overcomes. With his aspiration of sitting on the throne now realized, the Superhero is awakened unexpectedly out of his arrogant stupor, not by the chants of victory, but to the explicit rants of the next opponent in a long line of challengers against whom he will have to defend his title. In his defense of his crown, will the Superhero, display the resilience of a champion like Floyd 'Money' Mayweather, or will he will fail in his next battle after winning the title like Busta Douglass or after Tyson, to Antonio Tarver after Roy Jones, Jr.? After lusting for years after the distorted perception of an idea that mistakenly characterizes an image of what a champion is supposed to be, this novice champion becomes paralyzed in the exposure of the moment, movably shaken by the insurmountable pressure that calls into question the work ethic identified within his body of work. In order for a champion to continue to compete confidently at the high level to which he has excelled, he must develop an intense work ethic that will enable him to strengthen certain spiritual disciplines that will help him to maintain his poise under pressure.

A champion's personal dedication or lack thereof to his craft is the unchartered area to which most heroes never discipline themselves to excel. This creates a divide between his evolution from average to superstardom. Admiration for biblical champions like Joseph, Moses, Joshua, Nehemiah, David, Daniel, Hosea, and Job may have been nullified without the resilient and formidable display of consistency within the regimented discipline of each of these phenomenal superheroes while bearing up under the weight of attacks that came without warning.

Desire is what motivates champions to pursue after victory, but discipline is what is needed for the preservation of the reward they have obtained after their pursuit. It is all about the discipline to win and the consistency to perform at a high level of performance, whether on top or in distress, that causes even a leader's haters to approach him in battle respectfully because of his resolve in victory. In Philippians 4:11-13, the apostle Paul says it like this:

> *"I am not saying this because I am in need for I have learned to content whatever the circumstances. I know what it is to be in need, and I know what it is to have plenty. I have learned the secret of being content in any and every situation, whether well fed or hungry, whether living in plenty or want. I can do all things through Him who gives me strength"* (Philippians 4:11-13 (NIV))

In this context, the word "content" means "self-sufficient." In Stoic philosophy, the Greek word "contentment" described a person who dispassionately accepted whatever circumstances brought. For the Greeks, this contentment came from personal sufficiency, but for Paul contentment could only be found in the true source of his strength, Christ. Is the person the Superhero proclaims he is in victory the same person he is under pressure? Are you? Do you maintain your integrity while standing under the umbrella of desperation that seems to shield you from all relief? Or do you allow the flow of the circumstances around you to manipulate you into openly expressing your instability derived from your double mindedness? The apostle Paul makes this point very clear for both the leaders of his time and for future leaders that longevity in leadership is determined by a leader's discipline to continue to always be the same person all the time. As the Miami Heat, who continued to mature in the era of a champion, prepared to take on the San Antonio Spurs in the 2013 NBA Championship, the 2012 MVP,

LeBron James, has epitomized the discipline of winner on the other side of victory. What is most amazing about the resilience of the King James is his ability to adjust under pressure and how he continues effortlessly to display publicly a performance that reflects the tireless hours of hard work he has put in during the silent hours of the night where character is refined.

In the pursuit of leading the Miami Heat to winning back-to-back NBA titles, James, after a brutal seven game series against the inexperienced Indiana Pacers, was faced with the daunting task of defeating a champion to whom he had lost before, the San Antonio Spurs. The stage was set for the leaders of the new school to face the leaders of the old school in what was the battle of the ages. LeBron, like Adam, who due to his inexperience and immaturity failed to lead his team, Eve, to victory when challenged by the subtle, cunning, and wise skepticism of the influenced serpent, was awarded a second chance to avenge a title lost to an opponent maybe more disciplined than he. This time, however, he for the first time was playing from the posture of a champion and not a challenger.

After getting blown out by thirty-six points to the Spurs in game 3, the Heat was down 2-1 in a 7 game series, and played miserably in the first 3 games, both critics and fans alike began to ask, "Where is LeBron?" Where is the four time MVP of the League? When is the not One, not Two, not Three, not Four, not Five, not Six, not Seven-championship announcer going to step up? Where is the most unguardable, unstoppable, and what some presume to be the best player in the world? Who, and where, is the real LeBron James? In light of his victory, both critics and fans of the Superhero also begin to ask these same questions. Where is the Superhero? Where is the Godly hero who on the other side of victory continuously upholds his integrity after officially being announced the champion. Where and when is the Superhero, the people's champ, who has fallen and struggled to get up, going to take responsibility for his indiscretions and insert back into the history of his story those failures he purposely excommunicated from his life that proved to be memorials that lead to his success? Where is the Superhero? Is he dead? Is he still alive? If he is not dead and as Mr. Brown would say, "Yet Alive," then please ***Stand Up***! An APB has been put out, and a demand has been placed on the Superhero, the reigning champion, to ***Stand*** and ***Rise Up*** to the occasion. So on the other side of victory and in the words of Eminem, aka Slim Shaddy, "***Will the Real Superhero Please Stand UP?***"

Chapter Four

Will the Real Superhero Please Stand UP?

Who am I? A universal question that staggers the momentum of leaders around the world has caused many to fathom within their mind a definition of themselves that reflects their emotional instability. In the unethical, immoral, and rebellious societies we live in and try to police today, people have determined to give their life meaning based on how they feel rather than on the basis of whom God said they should be. This anti-Christian thought derived from the German philosopher, Soren Kierkegaard, who in the 1800's formulated a new way of thinking called Existentialism. This viewpoint denies that there is any truth or ultimate reality and, therefore, says that man must make his own meaning for his life. In the early twentieth century, Germany began to use these ideas to influence their people, ultimately leading to the beginning of World War II.[1] Rather than asking, "Who am I," the question should be, "Whom have I allowed to define me?" According to Webster's Dictionary, the word "define" means the determining of the outline, character, or limits of anything.

For some time, the posture of the Superhero's portfolio has been continuously redefined by the uncontrolled emotions of a culture determined to rebel against the original purpose for which Superheroes were created and continue to exist. Just think about it for a minute, when a manufacturer creates a product for customer use, they never, after having calculated in advance the possibilities of its failures, defects and malfunctions, allow customers to redefine the original purpose for which it was created and should be used. As a matter of fact, real inventors file a provisional patent or nondisclosure agreement for their invention, so that no other party can legally steal and then redistribute their invention for any other purpose or resell their product under another name.

Producers provide customer with the purposes for why the product was created, directions on how to use it, and the impending dangers that will come if the product is used incorrectly. Unfortunately, most consumers never read the directions, and endanger themselves and others by using the invention incorrectly. Instead of taking responsibility for their misuse of what the inventor has provided, they blame the manufacturer for the failure and use of a product they have applied ignorantly. As I said before, wisdom is the ability to see a thing in whatever capacity God created it in, and not to expect it to be anything more of less than what God said it should be. God has unmistakably, unrepentantly, and unchangeably defined everything once and for all within the confines of the purpose He created. Therefore, a Superhero is defined by his creator, God, equipped specifically and only for the purpose He saw fit.

The Superhero is an inventor's masterpiece created for customer use, an invention with a clearly defined purpose, directions on how to use, and warnings of the imminent danger that will come if used incorrectly. The rights to the Superhero brand, the tangible expression of the manufactures idea, are protected by the testimony of the Holy Spirit, the only eye witness wise enough to continue to authentically reveal to the world the true meaning of the Superhero the same way all the time. Like the diminishing meaning of a word translated from one language to another loses some of its value due to the various meanings of that word when defined within different cultural settings, the original meaning of the Superhero has been suppressed by the ignorance of translators who have left the interpretation of his meaning up to an audience trained in eisegesis rather than exegesis. Instead of drawing out the Superhero's purpose according to the origin of his overall context and discovering his meaning as defined by his creator, Exegesis, spectators redefine him in such a way that introduces their own presuppositions, agendas and biases into their interpretation of his meaning, Eisegesis. As a result of this unfortunate and unwarranted recalibration, the origin of the Superhero past has become a long lost memory in the imagination of a generation that has manipulated his meaning by configuring a Frankenstein recreation of his identity to defend the unrealistic expectation of the monster they presently call a real Superhero. Although there should be no difference between the two, the distance that separates the residue of the Superhero's past from the fantasy of his present is the confusion that causes both haters and appreciators of the Superhero Saga to ask, "Will the Real Superhero Please Stand UP?"

So after the Superhero has done all he can, successfully making it through an intensely hostile interview, and experiencing life on the other side of victory, all that is left for him to do is to STAND! Standing, however, is not as easily done as it may sound. Similar to salvation— God delivering humanity from the consequences of sin and death by devoting humanities' attention to an alternative greater than what they were delivered from—standing requires the Superhero to get up, balance his weight, and maintain a continuously forward walking motion on the path his creator defined for him. So will the real Superhero please STAND UP?

As the Superhero continues on his journey from a nobody to a "Superstar," the paparazzi begins to do a thorough background check to discover if he really has what it takes to be whom they want him to be.

Under the intense scrutiny of the media, the Superhero seeks to find, or possibly even create some controversial dilemma that will intrigue viewers to keep up with him through the various social media outlets. On his Twitter account, the Superhero writes to all his current and prospective followers, after experiencing life on the other side of victory, "I don't really need no new friends." After years of sitting quietly on the bench, never once throughout the tenure of his career ever catching the attention of any of the mass media outlets, the Superhero is constantly harassed by the sarcastic sentiments of fans singing, "We don't want no scrub."

The Superhero has emerged into an up and coming star, changing his status from off the bench to starter. Unaccustomed to the attention and high praise of being named a starter, he like so many other novices, who have found themselves in the same position, has had to learn how to maintain his composure when confronted with the daily analogies, critiques, and praises of his performance night in and night out. In most professions, unfortunately, most starters gracefully display a supernatural ability to master their craft when the lights are on, but they surprisingly display a lack of that mastery when they, in the words of my boy, Teddy Pendergrass, "Turn off the Lights." Now, from the dark shadows of an unrevealed past to a life filled with the allure of fame, money, and beautiful women who know he is in a much better position to make it rain rather than to make it drizzle, this question, so elegantly stated in a song performed by the former R&B

group Escape, arises, "When I need love who can I run to?" The difficulty at this level of figuring out the gold diggers from the genuine love of a true friend becomes more complex.

Real superheroes understand that the people they keep around them are the mirrors they use to reflect for themselves an image of the person they really are, but not necessarily the person they are supposed to be. At this point, the Superhero is faced with the daunting reality of getting up, balancing his weight, and maintaining that continuously forward walking motion around people whose lifestyle preaches wrong is right, right is wrong, making the pleasure of sin very appealing and easily accessible. Each of the three dimensions of standing mentioned above is arranged in order, requiring the cooperation of every phase to assure the firmness of his stance.

The first phase, Getting Up, is essential in the Superhero's evaluation of his recovery from falling, highlighting his humility to lean on the right source of strength he needs to reposition himself to stand under an evenly weighted foundation, rooted and grounded in the glamour of his success and the embarrassment of his sin. Getting Up, similar to restoration, is not only the physical repositioning of a fallen Superhero back into the upright posture from which he had fallen, but also the emotional and spiritual maturity, the blueprint, which will continue to remind him on how to get up, if and when he should fall again. The consummation of the Superhero's restoration is not complete when he Gets Up, because getting up does not guarantee he possess the strength necessary to stand without the support of others. Clearly, restoration is not picking up the Superhero that has either been moved or fallen from his place, and setting him in a place he had never been before, but rather picking him up, setting him back in the place where he was, and making him better than what he was before his fall. Likewise, when humanity fell, God sent His son Jesus, not for humanity to remain under the same impoverished condition to which it had tumbled, but to remind humanity of whom they were and empower the human race to plant their feet more securely in the same place from which they had once stood. In Scripture, we see this continuously revealed, especially in the story of the prodigal son:

> *"Not long after that, the younger son got together all that he had, set off for a distant country and there squandered his wealth in wild living. After he had spent everything, there was a severe famine in that whole country, and he begin to be in need. So he went and hired himself out to a citizen of that country, who sent him to his fields to feed pigs. He longed to fill his stomach with the pods that the pigs were eating, but no one gave him anything. WHEN HE CAME TO HIS SENSES, he said, How many of my father's hired servants have food to spare, and here I am starving to death! I will set out and go back to my fathers and say to him: Father, I have sinned against*

> *heaven and against you. I am no longer worthy to be called your son; make me like one of your hired servants. So he got up and went to his father. But while he was still a long way off, his father saw him and was filled with compassion for him; he ran to his son, threw his arms around him and kissed him"* (Luke 15:13-20 (AMP)).

Because of his premature exit from the comforts of his father's protection into a life filled with pleasure that promised things it could never satisfy, the prodigal son, after coming to his senses, returns to the place from which he willingly removed himself. To show his remorse for his riotous behavior, he returns under the impression that he is no longer worthy to be a son, and decides that he would rather be with his father as a hired hand than live in this world without his provisions. Although he no longer feels qualified to be a son, while he was still a long way off, his father runs to meet him where he is and, once there, he not only receives him but restores him back into the familiar posture of his sonship. It is interesting to note that even though the son no longer believes he is qualified to stand again in the shoes made for him, his father reminds him that even while falling he continued to wait for him to return to his vacant office.

God never disqualifies the Superhero when he falls, but meets him where he is, always reminding him of the hero he is even when he thinks the shoes he once wanted to wear are a size too big. In a similar fashion, the Get UP of the Superhero requires him to stand on the testimony of the good and the bad he has done in order to fulfill the responsibility of the next step within this trilogy, maintaining his balance.

Now standing in an upright position, the Superhero will have to relearn how to function under the burden of the weight he has been created to carry. Will he ever be able to stand comfortably, as an immovable presence, without the slightest blow of the wind knocking him down again after getting up? As he anxiously waits behind the curtain, eager to take the court in what will be his debut game as a starter, on his approach through the tunnel where thousands of fans are expecting nothing less than a championship, he begins in the words of Steve Arrington to get weak at the knees. As he takes the floor, the intensity in the arena buckles him, causing him to stumble and his coaches to question whether they made the right decision.

The Superhero, after considering the scrutiny he has had to endure as a bench player and his history of falling and getting back up, is confident that he will be able to maintain and excel in the weight class in which he currently finds himself. Balancing his weight requires the Superhero to manage his abilities within the context of time he has been given and to make the necessary adjustments to continue to produce steady results, even when faced with the inexperience of life situations while at the same time remaining steady in his character. It is important to first recognize that time is a weight God has placed on the Superhero, a weight that he, himself, cannot manage. Real superheroes do not try to manage time, because as the song says, "Time Keeps on Ticking, Ticking into the Future!" Instead of trying to manage time, an element in our universe controlled by God, they focus their energy on controlling their efforts within the context of time. Because time never stops, the old adage, "I just don't have enough time to...," is an excuse superheroes have used for years to dismiss themselves from carefully prioritizing the load of all life's other weights (God, family, etc.). Uncertain about how long this moment will last or if whether he will ever get the opportunity to be a starter again, the Superhero recognizes that, yes, now is the time, but that, in this moment, it is his responsibility to drop it like it is hot!

After the joys and stresses of an up-and-down season and having never been in this situation before, the Superhero becomes overwhelmed with the uncertainty of tomorrow because of the inexperience of his yesterday. Inexperience is a weight that gives the Superhero no verifiable grounds to be confident in what he thought he knew. This is an attribute that is usually found in a young superhero. Knowing a lot more than what has been experienced is the one thing that can minimize the Superhero's ability to approach his next challenge with the assurance of victory. Similarly, knowing about Jesus and knowing Jesus for yourself is not the same thing.

Most of the Superheroes in the faith only know about Jesus based on what another trusted confidant has told them about Him, but probably more that 80 percent have never once had an encounter or experience with Him for themselves. When the apostle Paul, a Superhero in the faith, encountered Jesus on the road to Damascus, his life changed. All that Paul, Saul at the time, thought he knew meant nothing after he experienced for himself the reality of what he was confident in thinking he had already known. All Superheroes must know and understand that knowledge is power, and the ignorance of the unlearned has caused many to qualify with their faith card to walk throughout life without making memorials that remind them of the knowledge they acquired through experience. In 1 Samuel 17, David says it like this:

> *"...When a lion or a bear came and carried off a sheep from the flock, I went after it, struck it and rescued the sheep from its mouth. When it turned on me, I seized it by its hair, struck it and killed it. Your servant has killed both the lion and the bear; this uncircumcised Philistine will be like one of them..."* (1 Samuel 17:34-36 (NIV)).

Through his experience with the lion and the bear, David gained the assurance of a successful tomorrow by leaning on the experience of his yesterday. The Superhero must always balance the weight of today by leaning on the memorials of yesterday's experiences. With this balance, he will be able to do a two-step on to maintaining a continuously forward walking motion on his life's journey of rediscovery.

The third and last of the three dimensions of Stand is the preservation of right conduct. The difficulty of rediscovering an answer to the question, "Who am I," has become even more tricky with his newfound fame. As a novice, a new convert into this luxurious and demanding life, the Superhero looks to cope with his inconsistencies on the court by indulging in the forbidden delicacies set up at the table of fame, during his down time off the court. Tempted to lust after distractions—sex, money, and drugs—so easily accessible on the other side of fame, he must choose to either conform to the ways of this world or display a higher level of resolve when it comes to the legacy that will forever be associated with his name. Here again, the apostle Paul explains it in Romans chapter twelve like this:

> *"I urge you, brothers and sisters, in view of God's mercy, to offer your bodies as a living sacrifice, holy and pleasing to God—this is your true and proper worship. Do not conform to the pattern of this world, but be transformed by the renewing of your mind"* (Romans 12:1-2 (AMP)).

The sexiness of the world and the pleasures it promises but never provides are the appealing alternatives that slowly breakdown the Superhero, piercing his core character values with a self-inflicted wound from which other superheroes have been unable to recover. If he surrenders to the seduction of this distraction, then he will prolong, or maybe even forfeit, his right to rediscover the real Superhero he is. Will the Superhero maintain his composure and continue to hold fast to those principles he has lived by all his life? Or will he take a dive on to the dark side, party like a rock star, and gain the whole world and lose his soul? It is evident that the true identity of the Real Superhero is an unusual site for sore eyes. Many have searched all over and could not find anybody; they have looked high and low, and still could not find anybody to represent the true identity of the Superhero. The Real Superhero, however, does not need to be defined, created, or found, but he does need to be rediscovered. The ignorance of his existence must not be used as a reason to excuse his absence from the human imagination. For whether one believes or not in his existence, that will never nullify the fact that he lives.

Within each one of us is a Superhero that is waiting to be rediscovered. That is right, the Real Superhero lives in you, and he is waiting for you to set him free. You loose him and let him go. Let him live and reflect through you a perfect image of your God, an image that only God can define Himself. So, I ask you again, and this time I strongly urge you to reply with your actions and not just your words, Will the Real Superhero Please Stand UP? Due to the magnitude of this request, employed within the configuration of these pages is the confession of a phenomenal Superhero, a confession that will object to every formidable excuse one might use to justify their reasons for not standing. So now, I present to you, in this the final chapter, I AM HIPSTAR: The Untold Story of A Phenomenal Superhero!

Chapter Five

I Am HIPSTAR: The Untold Story of a Phenomenal Superhero!

Phenomenal—the adjective derivative of phenomenon, a noun, which is defined as a fact, occurrence, or circumstance observed or observable; something that is impressive or extraordinary; a remarkable or exceptional person, prodigy, and/or wonder.[1] A Superhero can be defined as you, me, or any individual endowed with an inhumane, supernatural ability to stand in between the forces of evil and fight for the reemergence of the greater one residing in the bosom of those who have yet to rediscover the countenance of their gallant warrior leader ready to be released from the grips of the corruptible flesh. A Phenonenal Superhero, therefore, can be anybody, no matter what their deficiencies, handicaps, addictions, or mistakes, gifted with a plethora of extraordinarily unique superhuman abilities that enable their once disguised hero to heroically intervene on God's behalf for others facing the overwhelming temptations of a relentless evil, demanding the real Jesus hero in the afflicted to stand up and fight.

Within the contextual scope of this chapter is the story of an everyday average Joe, a hero just like you and me, graced with a supernatural ability to compel all people, despite his own struggles, to wholeheartedly surrender their will and their lives to his Lord and Savior, Jesus Christ. To all Superheroes, his story will serve as a reminder to us all to allow the hero in us to live today, lest your time on this earth prematurely expires. This is the real-time testimony of a Superhero gone too soon. This is the unheard confession, silenced by the unempathetic posture of those demanding an exceedingly abundant supply of their unique talents, as viewed through the eyes and life experience of this phenomenal Superhero. I consider it a great honor and privilege for God to have graced me with the opportunity to write this, my first biographical sketch entitled, "I Am HipStar: The Untold Story of A Phenomenal Superhero!"

Ladies and gentlemen, get up out of your seats, stand to your feet, and give it up for one of Hip Hops most undiscovered prodigies, the still, even in his death, undisputed heavyweight champion in the rap game today, a lyrical mastermind who for years packed out venues, subliminally ministering the message of Jesus Christ into the subconscious of both his fans and his Player Haters. The calculated consistency of his lyrical content left microphones consumed with a Holy fire, fueled by his extraordinary ability to proceed continuously to "Rock the Mic Right." So, get up out of your seats! I said you better Get Up! Everybody get up! If you haven't heard, I urge you to listen to the sound of real Hip Hop! To all my thugs, "Put your lighters up!" To every believer, "Lift your Bibles up!" Ladies and gentlemen, it is my honor to introduce to some and reveal to others, all the way from New Jersey baby, the untold story of a fabulously phenomenal Superhero. So get up out of your seats and give it up for my little brother, Branden Johnson, aka, ***MR. HIP, HIP, HIP-STARRRRRRRRRR!***

Like the extinguished flame of a microphone, soaked with the watered down lyrics of an MC formally gifted with an extraordinary ability "to rock the mic right," the beauty of an eternal flame once ignited by the fire of a Superhero's charisma is now daunted with the idolatrous kiss of his betrayer, who zealously seeks after the opportunity to sabotages the content of his Superhero's character. As the sun sets and the darkness begins to penetrate the sky, asserting its will, conditioning the atmosphere to accommodate its desire, the Superhero's saga is abruptly disrupted by the attempted murder of his hero by the ever existing presence of his internally evil Judas. On August 14, 2012, at approximately 11:31 P.M., the world stood still and time stopped ticking, both silenced by the stillness of a Superhero's unexpected death. Paralyzed in the surprise of the moment, loved ones, fans, and even his haters expeditiously converged onto the scene, only to discover that the facts reported prior to their arrival were true: Branden (HipStar) Johnson, a superhero to the residents of New Jersey, like Superman was to Metropolis or Batman to Gotham City, was gone.

As loved ones and fans gathered and united to console one another, forced to embrace the reality of life in the absence of the Superhero's presence, the silence was broken by the overwhelmingly lethargic shouts of "Branden, NOOOOOOOO!, and GOD WHY, WHY?," contaminating the atmosphere with an unjustified rationale commonly used to explain the cause for their losses. As the tragedy of their loss began to set in, some speculated that the reason why they were there was because God decided it was his time, excusing the Superhero from the responsibility of the choices and decisions he made by suggesting that the events that led up to and ultimately caused his demise were the inevitable realities of God's perfect will. The truth of why, however, can never be confirmed by the testimony of fans obsessed with the posture of his celebrity; why can only be answered through the testimony of the unconditional love of his loved ones, the main and most influential characters strategically positioned throughout the duration in the history of his story. Those individuals to which, if he could shower them with a song of praise, he would sing, *"They Loved Me through My Good and They Loved Me through My Bad."* In an attempt to publicly express the magnitude of their love for the beloved Superhero, by showcasing for the presumed audience an exaggerated display of their uncontrolled emotions, fans cried profusely at his funeral. For a moment, they displayed their appreciation for the talent of the entertainer he was. The hearts of his loved ones still long to feel his touch today, and continue to mourn daily in honor of the beautiful person the world will never be able to see he had become.

So just who was Branden 'Mister HipStar' Johnson? Branden Kelly Johnson, born on a cold snowy morning in January 1981, in the rough and tough city streets of Camden, New Jersey, was God's minstrel, a musician anointed with a melodious composition of songs that caused evil spirits resting on the afflicted to flee, replacing their heaviness with a Jesus labored rest. Yes, Bran, aka Mr. Hip, Coobie, or Hypnosis, was a revolutionary, a pioneer of the 21st century Jesus Christ campaign, inspiring through written word and his impeccable lyrical impressions, young and old, rich and poor, the happy and the hurting, the right and the wrong to come to know Jesus right know. He, through his Superhero powers, to which he was endowed with by the Creator, serenaded the world subliminally with the details of his life story, capturing the rhythm of his heart beat ministered through lyrics written in the high and valley low times of his life. He moved people to change not only in his life, but even more so in his death. Over 50 people committed their lives to Jesus during his homegoing service.

Branden was the partially damaged but durable canvas that God used to paint a picture of himself, a picture that rendered an authenticated expression of

God's heart's desire, love, and compassion towards those with whom HIP made contact. The picture, however, unless carefully examined under the revelation of Godly interpretation reflected, for some of the pioneers associated with HIP because of his artistry, a distorted perception of God's attitude towards them because of their obsession with maintaining the integrity of the partially damaged canvas on which it was painted. Like every other Superhero gifted with extraordinary capabilities hidden under the fragility and weakness of the human flesh, this superstar at times indulged publically with peers in celebratory sessions hosted by a plethora of illegally influential elements that stimulated the mind of his rebellious personality.

The 31 year old son, brother, friend to all, one of the original founders of the Young Brother Hood, better known as YBH, father of three, and fiancé to the one and only woman God blessed with the resource, will, and strength to love him the way God knew he needed to be loved, was a young Superhero. He aspired to make the world a better place, pontificating through the expression of music the intensity of his pain, suffered in the silence of those reaching to touch the hem of his fame, without ever embracing him with the necessary resolve that would relieve him from a life of worry and distress.

The Superhero, similar to Jesus in Matthew 9:20-22, who though touched by many, only turned to acknowledge the sincere embrace of a woman with an issue of blood, drew people, who declared their friendship when the spotlight was bright, but had a reputation of never coming to visit the Superhero when he called for them to join forces with him to fight a fight he could not win by himself. How hurtful could it be that after Branden had touched and been touched by so many, that he, from the recipients of his anointing, would never really experience an exchange of care for his pain after turning around and extending a helping hand to rescue them out of a fiery hell.

Where were all the fans who continued to stand in disbelief long after his body was lowered at the burial site, singing, "This is for my hommay," some nearly drunk, sipping up instead of pouring out liquor as an act of appreciation for their dead hero, when he, after giving in to the temporary pleasures of his struggle, screamed "Helpppppppp" while drowning in the misery of his failures? Where is the love now, the love promised by so many supposed-to-be friends for his dear mother and father who lost their beloved son, his sister Mo, his brothers Angello, Gino, Tony, and Nico, his nieces and nephews, and his real friends Sam, Troy, Fred, Brian, Life, and Shay, who attended with the utmost concern to the scars of his unhealed wounds, discovered once he decided to take off his Superhero costume and tuck away his cape?

To be clear, all superheroes long for the touch of the few individuals God anoints with the eyes to look in to them and see who has a desire to love them through their struggle and who is willing to bear with them in the continual battle to overcome a weakness. So just like

King David, whose desire to build God a house was methodically passed on to his beloved son Solomon, the successor to his throne, Branden was the conductor of an orchestrated symphony, colorfully composed with the rhythmic melody of an incomplete song waiting for the real superheroes to STAND UP and render an authentic expression through their performance of a song he left for them to sing.

Within the heart of every Superhero, there is the completion of a song left undone, a song he left for only his true successors to finish. It is important to note in this juncture of the book, that the wealthiest place in the world is not Hollywood, but the graveyard, where the tombstones of millions of unknown superheroes have been mounted to honor the memory of soldiers who have left this world prematurely. Buried in these caskets, plunged down six feet into the core of the earth, are songs that were never sung, books that were never written, inventions that were never created, businesses that were never opened, ideas that never became reality, paintings that were never painted, music that no one has ever heard, and visions that ended as nightmares. Graveyards all over the world are filled with the wealthiest people who have left this world without ever exhausting and relieving themselves of the identity of their Superhero within, leaving nothing worthwhile for their fans to remember them by.

A Superhero should always make it his number one priority to leave this world empty, leaving a legacy for his successors to continue to build from that point at which his work stopped. If a Superhero, however, exits this life prematurely the song he never sang, the business he never opened, the picture he never painted, and the ideas that never became reality become the burden for those who have captured his heart to render an expression that will forever remind future generations of his life contributions.

A real Superhero never dies, but he reproduces in others his desire to continue to pursue after the reality of a dream he introduced to the world. The Superhero's confession is articulated in the tune of a song he wrote, but intended for somebody else to sing. Jesus, the epitome of a real superhero, sang a song that inspired wounded leaders all around the world to rediscover their superhero within and demand for their hero within to sing. Have you rediscovered the Superhero residing in you? Have you allowed him to escape through the words of a song written by the greatest songwriter of all times? Have you even allowed your Superhero to exist, let alone sing? Even though Superheroes are singing the same song, due to the distinction in their voices and the difference in experience, they all will not sing this song the same way. When Superheroes sing the Jesus song, the world can still see their good and their bad, but they become one with Christ, making it impossible for the world to distinguish between the two of them.

Like an R&B classic, Branden's life is a masterpiece that has inspired others to finish the words to a song he never had a chance to finish. With the message of

Christ injected all throughout the anatomy of his music, HIP in this his last and probably most memorable performance, takes the stage one last time to confess to real superheroes all around world his last word through this poetic dissertation delivered in a way that only Branden could do:

> "Listen, HipStar in the building; better get it right. I counted five, but all I really need is one mic. Gone, but still these MC's want to test me, call in question my ethics and my integrity. It's HIP, still holding my position tight. I'm the champ; this is not my first time in a title fight. Listen, I know my situation complicated, but heaven is real. I praise God that I finally made it. Walking on these streets all paved in gold, rocking my victor's crown, and clothed in my white robe, I confess I'm a sinner. I'm not innocent; my efforts had nothing to do with me obtaining these benefits. But Christ, you know the one that bled and died for me, awarded me this time, cause can't nobody tell my story, like me, HIP.
>
> Those nights I sat, I prayed, I cried, asking God to explain, but He never ever answered me why, my body stimulated, mind got to contemplating, frustrated and I wasn't sure if I would even make it. What I chose, I can't change; and now I'm feeling badly, in this moment, I learn to depend on the love of my family. They love

me through my good and my bad. Let me introduce you to the family every Ssuperhero wish he had. Hey ya'll, forgive me. I'm sorry. I really miss you; wish I could reach down love, hug you, hold you, and kiss you, but I'm ok, because I know I'll see you all again. Living saved guarantees that you will have a chance to make it in. See, God's the Father every person wished they could have ever had; He's the epitome of everything that a real dad should be. When I fell, he helped me get back on my feet and stand. He explained to me the responsibilities of a real man, but Satan took me to the top of the mountain and then told me to dive; God's angels will catch you and surely you will not die.

So now, in heaven with my angel wings, I'm flying high. I announce to you Satan that YOU CAN NEVER TAKE MY JOY, YOU CAN NEVER STILL MY PEACE. YOU CAN NEVER TAKE THIS HAPPINESS I HAVE INSIDE. I'M SOLDIER; I GONNA RIDE!

Branden Johnson

Branden, your music continues to play in the hearts of all those who love you. We will open our hearts wide and sing loud for the whole world to hear the voice of the wonderful person singing behind the song we sing. We love you Branden and we miss you. We will make sure to let the world know that you truly were and still are a Phenomenal Superhero!

Book by the Author

The Wounded Leader

A Superhero Revealed
Through the Eyes of His Alter Ego

Available in retail stores, on www.amazon.com, www.barnes&noble.com, or wherever books are sold.

End Notes

Chapter Four

[1] Combee, Jerry H., Phd., *History of the World in Christian Perspective,* 3d ed. (Pensacola, Florida: A Beka Book Publications, 2005).

Chapter Five

[1] Phenomenal. Dictionary.com. Collins English Dictionary - Complete & Unabridged 10th Edition. HarperCollins Publishers. http://dictionary.reference.com/browse/phenomenal (accessed: 2013).

Contact Information

To inquire about Pastor Shaun Saunders speaking, ministering, or doing book signing and discussions at your event, you may contact him by writing to:

Pastor Shaun Saunders
2436 Brianna Dr.
Hampton, GA 30228

You may also send him an email at:

ssaunders89@yahoo.com

Connect with him on Twitter at:

www.twitter.com/ShaunSaunders3

www.ingramcontent.com/pod-product-compliance
Lightning Source LLC
LaVergne TN
LVHW050939080826
845145LV00004B/1333

* 9 7 8 0 6 9 2 0 2 2 4 4 3 *